Extracts from Zlata's Diary

Zlata Filipović

Zlata with her
diary

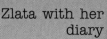

Acknowledgements
Photos: Sipa Press/Alexandra Boulat, cover, title page, pages 9, 10, 13, 19, 29.
Paul Lowe/Magnum Photos, pages 3, 6, 16, 24. Martin Mayer/Network, page 5. AFP EPA/A Niedringhaus,
page 22. Popperfoto/AFP, page 26.

Illustrations: M2, pages 30, 31.

Heinemann Educational Publishers
Halley Court, Jordan Hill, Oxford OX2 8EJ
a division of Reed Educational & Professional Publishing Limited
www.heinemann.co.uk

Heinemann is a registered trademark of Reed Educational & Professional
Publishing Limited

First published 2000
Original edition © Fixot et les Editions Robert Laffont, Paris, 1993. Published in French under the title **Le
Journal De Zlata**, originally published in English by Viking, 1994.
Literacy edition published in 1999
Literacy Satellite edition © Fixot et les Editions Robert Laffont, Paris, 2000
Additional writing for Satellites by Wendy Cobb

04 03 02 01
10 9 8 7 6 5 4 3 2

ISBN 0 435 11960 5   **Extracts from Zlata's Diary** single copy
ISBN 0 435 11964 8   **Extracts from Zlata's Diary** 6 copy pack

Designed by M2. Printed and bound in Scotland by Scotprint

You might like to learn more about Zlata by reading the full version of her diary.
It is published in the UK by Penguin, ISBN 0-140-37463-9
All information and borders on maps of former Yugoslavia are correct at time of going to press.

Introduction

Zlata Filipovic started her diary in September 1991. She was 10.

She called her diary Mimmy and wrote in it as if she was talking to her best friend.

When she started her diary, Zlata lived like any other 10 year old. She had enjoyed a lovely summer holiday and was looking forward to seeing her friends at school.

But soon, life changed. Zlata lived in Bosnia-Herzegovina (see the map on page 31) and a war started there between different groups of people. As we read her diary, we can feel how scary the war was for children like Zlata.

When fighting started in her city, Sarajevo, her life was turned upside down. Her school was closed and she lost contact with her friends. She had to hide in cellars with her family and it was not safe to walk in the streets in case she was shot.

It was terrible. As Zlata says in her diary, 'I feel as though no one and nothing here will survive.'

Brian Moses

Zlata's friends and relations

You will meet these people in Zlata's diary:

Alicia – her mother

Bobar family – they live next door to her and are very good friends

Braco – a friend of her parents

Keka – Braco's wife

Cicko – her canary – a small bird in a cage

Malik – her father

Neda – her mother's friend at work

Srdjan – another friend of her parents

Monday, 2 September 1991

At last the summer holidays are over and today we go back to school. I'll be going up into the fifth grade.

I'm longing to see all my friends again. I haven't seen some of them since the last day of last term. My best friend is Mirna. It'll be fun when we're all together again.

Sarajevo in 1991

Sunday, 6 October 1991

I'm watching the American top 20 on the telly. I've just had a Four Seasons pizza with ham, cheese, mushrooms and ketchup. It was yummy!

I've been working so hard on my homework — all weekend! I didn't even go to the park with my friends. I just worked, worked, worked! So I should get a good mark at school tomorrow.

Zlata writing her diary at home in Sarajevo

Wednesday, 23 October 1991

The news from the town of Dubrovnik is terrible. We see horrible pictures on the telly. The people who live there have no water, no electricity and no phones. They are living in bomb shelters.

Mummy and Daddy are very upset. Mummy says it is such a beautiful town. And it's where Mummy and Daddy got married.

Mummy and Daddy's best friend, Srdjan, works in Dubrovnik. We are all worried sick about him. His wife is here, in Sarajevo, and she can't get any news about him because Dubrovnik is cut off from the rest of the world.

Tuesday, 12 November 1991

Things are getting even worse in Dubrovnik!
The pictures we see on the telly are so scary.
People there are starving.

We have found out that Srdjan and his parents
are alive, so we are going to try to send them a
parcel. There's no post but some people in the
church can get them through.

Daddy is still going to train as a reserve
soldier. He gets so tired. We are so sick of this
war. Daddy says it might stop next week.
Thank God.

Thursday, 14 November 1991

Yes! Daddy isn't going to the reserves any more. Yippee! That means we can go away at weekends. But we have a new problem - no petrol. Daddy waits for ages to buy some but he doesn't always get it.

We managed to send a parcel to Srdjan. He and his parents have nothing to eat. It's even hard to get water. He swapped a bottle of whisky for a big bottle of water.

Zlata with her parents, Alicia and Malik

Monday, 2 December 1991

It's my birthday tomorrow! Mummy is making a cake because tomorrow I'm having my friends to my party. Mummy and I are making a tombola and thinking up a quiz for the children. It will look lovely because the party plates and cups have little apples all over them. And the cake is like a butterfly. I'll have to take a deep breath to blow out eleven candles!

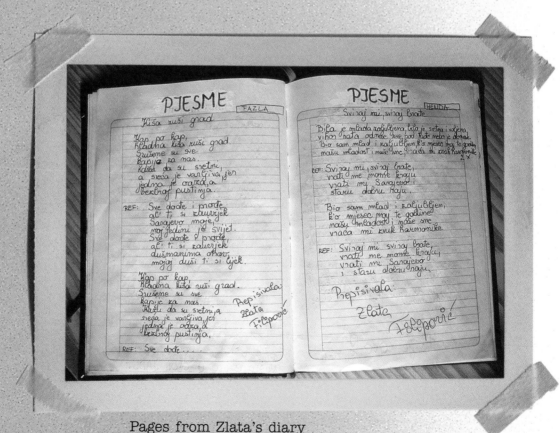

Pages from Zlata's diary

Thursday, 19 December 1991

When we sent the parcel to Srdjan we put
another parcel inside it. It was for him to give
to a child in Dubrovnik. There were
- sweets
- chocolates
- vitamins
- a doll
- books
- pencils
- notebooks.

I hope it makes some child happy. Because of
the war the children in Dubrovnik can't go to
school, can't play with their friends and can't
get enough to eat.

I also put a New Year's card in it saying I
hope the war will soon be over.

Tuesday, 14 January 1992

I'm listening to the music from 'Top Gun' on the radio.
 I've just had a chat with Mummy on the phone. She's at work.
 Every night I dream that I ask Michael Jackson for his autograph. But I never get it. Poor me!

Tuesday, 4 February 1992

School has started and now I have to go to music school, as well. It's OK.
 I'm sticking photos of famous models in a note book. I've got pictures of Linda Evangelista, Claudia Schiffer, Cindy Crawford and Yasmin le Bon.

Thursday, 5 March 1992

Oh God! Things are getting bad here. Last Sunday, there was a wedding. Some people killed one of the guests.
 The next day the city was full of barricades. There were 1,000 of them so no one could get anywhere and we didn't even have any bread. By 6 o'clock people got fed up and went out into the streets. People marched in a long line through the streets of Sarajevo. They shouted words like 'We'll live together!' and 'Come and join us!'

Zlata behind a barbed wire barricade

Friday, 6 March 1992

Things are back to normal.

Monday, 30 March 1992

I've had an idea, Diary! When Anne Frank wrote her diary, she called it Kitty, and pretended it was her best friend. So I'm going to call you – let me think – I know – Mimmy!
  OK, then, here goes.

Dear Mimmy,

It's nearly half-term and we are all working hard for our tests.
  Tomorrow we were supposed to be going to a concert in a big hall in town. But our teacher says it could be dangerous. Somebody might put a bomb in the hall.
  Mummy thinks so too, so I'm not going.

Love,

Zlata

Sunday, 5 April 1992

Dear Mimmy,

My homework is reading, but I just can't concentrate.

Something is going on in town. We can hear gunfire coming from the hills. We can tell that something really scary is going to happen. I can see lots of people on the telly. They are meeting outside the government buildings.

The radio keeps playing the same song: 'Sarajevo, My Love'.

My tummy hurts and I just can't do my homework.

Oh, Mimmy, I'm so scared of WAR!

Here is Zlata writing her diary by candlelight
after the electricity had been cut off.

Monday, 6 April 1992

Dear Mimmy

I told you, yesterday, that some people were in front of the
government building. Well, somebody shot at them! Nobody
knows who or why!

A student was KILLED. Her blood ran all over the road.
Her last words before she died were, 'Is this Sarajevo?'
HORRIBLE, HORRIBLE, HORRIBLE!
NO ONE AND NOTHING HERE IS NORMAL!

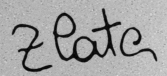

Thursday, 9 April 1992

Dear Mimmy,

I'm not going to school. All the schools in Sarajevo are closed. There's danger in the hills around the town. We can still hear some gunfire but the worst explosions have stopped.

Mummy and Daddy are not going to work. We're buying lots and lots of food.

It's very scary and Mummy is terribly worried. Daddy keeps trying to calm her down. She spends all her time on the phone, talking to friends and family.

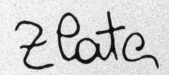

Tuesday, 14 April 1992

Dear Mimmy,

People are leaving our city. The airport is packed and so are the bus and train stations. On the telly I saw such sad pictures of people saying goodbye. Some are staying, some are going. It's so unfair. These people have done nothing wrong.

Our friends Keka and Braco came around this morning. They're whispering with Mummy and Daddy, in the kitchen. Mummy and Keka are crying.

I don't think they know if we should stay here or go. It's awful, whatever we do.

Saturday, 18 April 1992

Dear Mimmy,

Well, we're still here, and it's terrible. There's shooting and shells are falling. This is WAR!

Mummy and Daddy sit up late every night, worrying about what to do. Should we stay here together or split up? Keka wants to take me with her, away from Sarajevo. But Mummy can't make up her mind. She's crying all the time.

Everything is terrible, and the worst thing is that Mummy has packed my suitcase.

Love,

Zlata

Zlata and her parents with their cases packed, hoping to leave Sarajevo

Wednesday, 22 April 1992

Dear Mimmy,

We spent the whole night in the Bobars' cellar. We went there around 21:30 and came home at about 10:30 the next morning. I slept from 4:00 to 9:30 a.m. It boomed and shook really badly last night.

Zlata

Sunday, 26 April 1992

Dear Mimmy,

We spent Thursday night at the Bobars, again. When we got home we found we had no electricity.

We had no bread so Mummy had to bake some. It was the first time she had ever baked her own bread. But it tasted good!

I was supposed to be leaving Sarajevo that day, with Keka and her two girls. But none of us left.

Bye!

Your
Zlata

Saturday, 2 May 1992

Dear Mimmy,

Today was the worst day ever! When the shooting started I took Cicko [Zlata's canary] and went downstairs.

  The gunfire was so bad we couldn't get over the wall to the Bobars' house. So we had to run down to our own cellar.

  Our cellar is dark and smelly. We huddled in the corner, listening to the shells exploding and the guns. We even heard planes.

  Suddenly I realised that this awful cellar was keeping us safe and it started to look quite nice! I had to put my fingers in my ears to keep out the sound of glass breaking in our street. It was terrible.

  Bye!

Sunday, 3 May 1992

Dear Mimmy,

Daddy ran all the way to Grandma and Grandpa's house. Then he ran back to tell us they were OK, thank God. He was sweating and upset by what he had seen in town.

The main street is in a terrible mess. Shop windows are smashed, and so are cars and buildings.

Most people were lucky and found somewhere to shelter.

We talked to the Bobars a few minutes ago. Yesterday, when that awful shelling was going on, they were out in the street! They ran down into the cellar at their friend Stela's house.

Zlata

A Bosnian woman looking for her belongings after her house was bombed

Tuesday, 5 May 1992

Dear Mimmy,

The shooting seems to be dying down. I do not understand what this war is all about. I wish the politicians would sort it out and let us have PEACE! PLEASE!

   We've had to change things around in our flat. Our bedrooms face the hills where the shooting comes from. So we've put mattresses on the floor in a corner of the sitting room. It's weird! Cicko's been moved to the kitchen because it's safer there, but really, only the cellar is safe when the shooting starts.

   Bye!

Sunday, 17 May 1992

Dear Mimmy,

We now know for sure – NO MORE SCHOOL!
   Because of the war the schools have closed. Children spend their time in cellars instead of classrooms. We can't do our exams so the teachers will give us the same marks that we got at the end of last term. It's only May and I've finished fifth grade!

   Bye!
   Zlata

There was often no water in the houses. Zlata used to collect water in big, plastic bottles.

Wednesday, 20 May 1992

Dear Mimmy,

The shooting has died down so Mummy went to
see Grandma and Grandpa. She met lots of people
and then came back feeling miserable about all
their sad news.
 Six days ago her brother was wounded. She has
only just found out and she's very upset. And how
can she get to see him in hospital? He might as
well be at the other end of the world! They've told
her he's OK but she just keeps crying and saying,
'I won't believe it until I see him with my own
eyes.'

Monday, 25 May 1992

Dear Mimmy,

Today, the wonderful Zetra Hall went up in flames. All the world knew what a lovely building it was and now it's burning.

 The people who start wars don't know anything about love. They just know how to destroy. They take things away. So now they've taken away this lovely building, as well. It makes me feel so sad, Mimmy.

 I feel as though soon no one and nothing here will be left.

Your

Zlata

The biggest building in Sarajevo burnt down after a night of heavy shelling.

Wednesday, 27 May 1992

Dear Mimmy,

HORROR! BLOOD! SCREAMS! TEARS!

A shell exploded in the market. Mummy was near there at the time. Daddy and I didn't know where she was. We were beside ourselves, worrying about her.

I saw some of it on the telly. HORRIBLE! They started taking the wounded to hospital.

We kept going to the window to look for Mummy. Was she alive? At 4 o'clock Daddy said he was going to the hospital and I got ready to go to the Bobars. I looked out of the window one last time AND SAW MUMMY RUNNING TO THE HOUSE. She started shaking and crying when she got home. Everyone came to make sure she was all right. She told us about the bodies she had seen.

A HORRIBLE, UNFORGETTABLE DAY!

Thank God Mummy's with us.

Your

Saturday, 30 May 1992

Dear Mimmy,

The hospital where I was born has been burnt down. It was new but now it has gone. The mothers and the babies were saved.

People get killed here. People die here. People go missing here. Things go up in flames here. And out of it all come new little lives.

Your

Zlata

Here is Zlata in Paris. At last she could be a child again.

Afterword

Zlata went on writing her diary until 1993. Things got worse and they had no water, gas or electricity. In February 1993 she wrote, 'God, I keep thinking this is going to stop. But the war just goes on and on.'

It was Zlata's diary that helped the family to escape. A French firm published her diary and it was soon translated into 30 languages. Zlata and her family were taken to live in France. But Zlata has not forgotten the children left behind in Sarajevo. She said, 'I think of my little friend back home, who is four. She has no toys and has never known anything but war.'

The fighting went on until 1994. By then 10,500 people had been killed. The city of Sarajevo is still recovering from the horrors of war.

Brian Moses

How Zlata's world changed:
Yugoslavia before and after the war

Right: Yugoslavia's position in Europe.

Below: A map of Yugoslavia as it was in 1991/92, before the war.

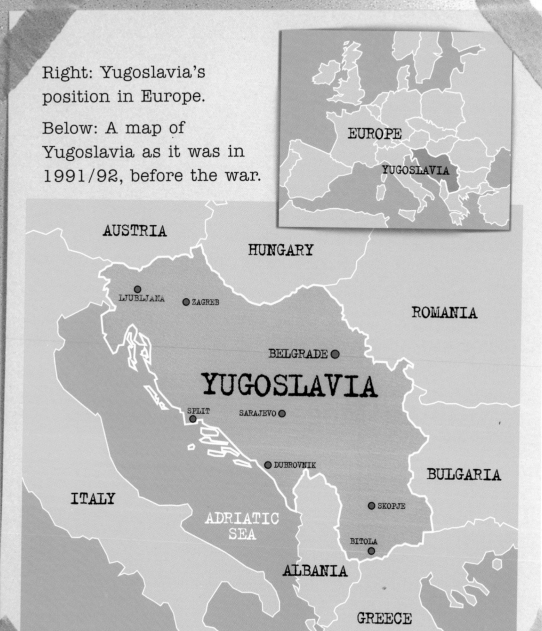

Below: Yugoslavia became SIX new countries – Slovenia, Croatia, Serbia, Montenegro, Macedonia and Bosnia-Herzegovina, where Zlata's family lived.

Index